sixty sermon illustrations

david adam

kevin mayhew

First published in 2005 by

KEVIN MAYHEW LTD
Buxhall, Stowmarket, Suffolk, IP14 3BW
E-mail: info@kevinmayhewltd.com
Web: www.kevinmayhew.com

Sixty Sermon Illustrations is extracted from *Searchlights*

9 8 7 6 5 4 3 2 1 0

ISBN 1 84417 489 1
Catalogue No 1500853

Cover design by Joseph Attard

Printed in Great Britain

Contents

Introduction

This book was compiled with the busy minister, preacher or speaker in mind: it can be a daunting task to find a fresh theme or topic each week and these short pieces will hopefully be a handy resource. They are meant to help provide that sometimes elusive topic or to amplify an existing central theme.

Visual aids often speak more directly than words and these short, vivid illustrations, as well as illustrations from your locality, can help you to throw light on the Scripture passages and to relate them to what is happening in your community or the world.

By referring to the two indexes (Topical and Bible reference) you can decide how to plan the sermon or expand on your own theme. The cross-referencing means that you have quite a few ideas at your fingertips.

1 Waiting for God

Aim

To make people more aware that Christ comes to them today.

Readings

Mark 13:35

Illustration

It was near Christmas and in the Advent season, and Peter waited for God to come. He prayed every day, 'God, show me your face and I shall be saved.' Peter had tried to live a good life; he was now old and looked forward to the coming of God. He continued to work in his paper shop, where he had worked most of his life. Here he heard all sorts of conversations and met many people. A single mum was telling a friend how she did not have enough money to buy presents for her child. When everyone else had gone, Peter said to her, 'I heard what you said. I have a few toys on the shelves; they are not selling very well, go and pick anything you would like.' She could hardly believe it for there were some wonderful things on the shelves. As she went away with her arms full, Peter was delighted. His reward was her smile.

Later that day, he caught a young lad stealing a magazine from the shelves. He was on the way out with the magazine up his jumper when Peter stopped him. He could have called the police or told the boy's parents. He saw the boy was poor and afraid, and he felt sorry for him. 'If you want a magazine, and have no money, talk with me,' he said. 'Magazines are soon out of date; I can always find one to give you. You must not just help yourself. Take the magazine for free and ask me another time.' The boy's face changed from a look of fear to a beaming smile. He thanked Peter and ran from the shop.

An old man came into the shop and was saying how lonely he was since his wife died. This would be his first Christmas on his own – he was not looking forward to it. Peter said, 'We were expecting a friend to come for Christmas, and he has said he cannot make it. We have prepared for his coming. Would you come to us instead? We would love to share Christmas with you.' The old man's face lit up in a beautiful smile and he said, 'You have made me feel so wanted, and I would love to come.'

That night Peter prayed his Advent prayer, 'Show me your face and I shall be saved.' In a dream God spoke to him and said, 'Peter, today I came to you, and three times you made me smile. Grace and peace be upon you.'

(Apologies to Tolstoy!)

2 Stir up Sunday

Aim
To show we need to prepare for the coming of our Lord.

Readings
Mark 1:3

Illustration
The Sunday before the beginning of Advent used to be called 'Stir up Sunday' for two reasons. The prayer for the Sunday begins, 'Stir up, O Lord, the wills of your faithful people'; a wonderful prayer that wants us to 'bring forth the fruits of good works'. It is by what we do that we will be known, so it is important that our works are good, important that we do something.

Traditionally 'Stir up Sunday' was also the time when the Christmas cake was made. Mother would get all the ingredients – the flour, the fruit, the eggs – and mix them together. Everyone in the house had a stir of the cake before it went into the oven. All this was part of the preparations before Christmas.

We now often spend weeks preparing for this one day. How much time do we spend preparing for the coming of God to us?

If someone is coming to stay, we will make sure there is room for them, that we have time for them, that we will give them some attention. Our God comes and seeks room in our lives; he wants us to be aware of him, for us to give him some of our time and attention.

Are you prepared for this?

3 Help is on the Way

Aim

To encourage people to see that Jesus comes in acts of kindness and righteousness.

Readings

John 1:9-13

Illustration

Once upon a time there was a man who went out to sea in a little boat. It was a lovely day and he was enjoying himself. Then the mist suddenly came down. Now he did not know which direction he was going in. He rowed around until he was very tired, then he let himself drift. He did not know that he was drifting towards the rocks. Suddenly he heard a crunch and a scraping. His boat was torn on the rocks and it began to sink. Fortunately he managed to escape on to the rocks. He was now very cold and hungry and he prayed to God to come and rescue him.

Soon a motorboat came by and invited him aboard – but he refused, saying, 'I have help coming.' A little later a fishing boat saw him and tried to persuade him to come off the rock but again he said, 'There is no need to worry I have help on the way.'

That night the man died alone in the cold. He went to heaven and complained to God that he had not come to help. God said, 'I came in a motorboat and you refused my help. I came again in a fishing boat and you still refused my help. You are here today because you did not recognise my help when it came – yet still you are loved.'

4 Ready for Christmas

Aim

To show God's kingdom comes when his will is done.

Readings

John 2:11
Luke 2:7

Illustration

Are you ready for Christmas? Have you sent all your cards? Bought presents? Got the food ready? What will you do on Christmas Day? Will you make room for Jesus: make sure Christ is in Christ-mas?

It was Jessie's birthday and she looked forward to it. She lived in an old people's home and had friends around her – but she was invited to her daughter's for her birthday. She would be with the family, including the three children. They made sure there was a nice room ready for her and the house was warm. Her daughter had bought the food she liked. All was ready.

On the first night her daughter had an evening class, the children were out with friends, and her son-in-law decided to go to the pub. On her birthday the children had other things to do and so would be out all day – football, swimming and netball are important. Jessie's son-in-law spent the day in the garage tinkering with his car, and her daughter decided to do some last-minute shopping on her own. Again Jessie was left alone. They had a meal together in the evening, then the children went on the computer and the others watched television. Jessie was glad to go back to the home where people had time to talk to her and give their attention to her.

Will we make time for Jesus on his birthday, or will we be too busy doing other things?

5 God's Gift

Aim

To rejoice that Jesus Christ has come into the world.

Readings

John 3:16

Illustration

Mother and Father had wrapped up the present in beautiful paper with tinsel and bows. The present was in a big box. For a long time it remained unopened as if their child was frightened of it. Then the paper was taken off and folded up carefully, the present was taken out of the box, and the child played the whole day with the box. The child enjoyed having the box and playing with it. Mother and Father hoped that their child would soon realise what a wonderful present had been given to her . . .

I knew an old lady who was uninterested in presents. Whenever she was given a present, she was very grateful. She always remembered to say, 'Thank you'. But she did not open the gift. In her house I saw a pile of unopened gifts and I felt it was rather strange and sad.

Today I would like to give you all a present of a cheque for one million pounds. But you can only have it on one condition: you are to frame it, to show how generous I am, but not cash it.

Let us get behind the tinsel and the wrappings today and discover God's greatest gift. He gives himself to us. Let us come and give ourselves to him.

6 Seeing Clearly

Aim

To show that the people involved in the birth of Jesus were ordinary people involved in an extraordinary event.

Readings

John 1:18

Illustration

Sally was naughty at school. She did not pay attention to what was written on the board, nor was she all that keen on being out in the country because she was not really interested in the flowers or the birds. A beautiful scene did not move her with joy. Starry nights did not fill her with awe. Then it was discovered that Sally was very short-sighted and needed glasses. She had not been able to see what was around her, so her world and her life were restricted by her vision. Once she had glasses the world became a place full of wonder and beauty. She loved going out into the country to enjoy the scenery, to watch the birds and see the flowers. Once Sally saw more clearly, her whole world changed.

7 A Free Gift

Aim
To encourage people to wonder at the mystery of Christmas.

Readings
Romans 6:23

Illustration
I get tired of letters through the door that say you have been especially chosen – I know that everyone is getting such a letter. Then it tells me I have won £10,000 – whoopee! But the small print says, 'if my number comes up', and the real chances of that are more than a million to one.

God is not like that. God's offer is not gifts (though he does offer us them); he offers himself to us in Jesus Christ our Lord. We do not deserve this; we cannot win it. God has chosen to give himself to us. All we have to do is accept his presence and his love.

8 Wise Men

Aim
To show how the Christ was revealed to all nations.

Readings
Matthew 2:1-12

Illustration
The wise men were not all that wise because they went to the wrong place and the wrong person. They went to the capital, Jerusalem, and to King Herod. Fancy asking him, 'Where is he who is to be born king of the Jews?' Herod hadn't a clue but he knew who would know about the Messiah, about the Christ. He asked the chief priests and scribes. They told him, 'In Bethlehem in the land of Judah.' Lucky for the wise men it was only about seven miles away. Herod sent them off and told them to search diligently for the child and to tell him when they had found him. Fortunately, the wise men did not trust Herod or his interest in the Christ child.

We assume there were three because we are told of three gifts. We know that they were rich, foreign and wise, but we do not know that they were kings. The shepherds were ordinary Jews smelling of sheep and probably not able to read or write. These men were different indeed, almost in total contrast. It helps us to see God calls all peoples to come to him – rich and poor, the known and the stranger, simple and wise; all are invited to come to God.

9 Full or Empty?

Aim

To encourage people to think about the Holy Trinity.

Readings

Acts 2:4
Romans 15:13

Illustration

Have a nice mug, which is empty. Get people to admire it, tell them how beautiful it is – but it is useless unless it has something in it – it is no use empty! Only when it has something in it does it fulfil its purpose. People and their minds are the same: we are no use if we are empty.

Borrow a jacket or a fleece, lay it before you and admire it. How good it is for keeping out the cold. Now command it to raise an arm or to sit up straight. When it fails to act, say you know a secret way of getting it to do things. Now get the owner to put it on and raise an arm. The jacket is of no use unless it is occupied.

Nature abhors a vacuum – something will always fill an empty space. Let us all be filled with the Holy Spirit of God.

10 Listening

Aim
To learn the value of listening.

Readings
1 Samuel 3:9

Illustration
Hello!
Are you receiving me?
Hello!
Are you receiving me?
Hello!
Are you receiving me?

This was a conversation, if you can call it that, on a mobile phone. The person was in a bad reception area. There was too much interference from hills and trees. They would have to go to a better reception area.

It is amazing how many people and nations are good at speaking but find it very hard to hear anyone. Our speakers (mouths) seem to be far more active than our receivers (ears). A proverb from the East says, 'God gave us two ears and one mouth so that we should listen twice as much as we speak.'

11 Abundant Life

Aim
To show that miracles are mysteries and signs of the kingdom.

Readings
John 10:10

Illustration
Have you ever heard of Dracula? Dracula is supposed to come when you are asleep and drain away your life. When you wake up in the morning you are at least half dead. It is not a true story but sometimes we can wake exhausted; we can feel we have no energy. Human resources do run out. Our batteries need recharging; we need to be refreshed and renewed.

When we feel we have reached the bottom of the barrel we need outside help. There are times when we are unable to help ourselves but Jesus is able to help us. In John 10:10, Jesus says, 'I came that they may have life, and have it abundantly.' You can trace this giving of abundant life, and how Jesus meets various needs and losses of well-being, in John's Gospel:

Need more wine – 2:1-11
Loss of well-being – 4:46-54
Lack strength – 5:2-9
Lack energy (food) – 6:1-14
Lack of security and safety – 6:16-21
Lack of vision and light – 9:1-7
Loss of life – 11:1-44

Jesus meets our drained resources with his generosity and power.

12 Light

Aim

To continue to show signs of the Christ.

Readings

2 Corinthians 4:6

Illustration

Show an array of lights.

An ordinary lamp is useful when the sun goes down for it helps us to see around the house in the dark. A torch is useful for it is the sort of light you can carry around with you and use whenever you need it. Laser light is used in hospitals for surgery and it is also used as a military weapon – laser always has to be used with great care. A security light is good to welcome you home and also to show up any intruders. People who like to sneak about in the dark do not like security lights – especially if linked with a burglar alarm.

The greatest light we have is the sun. Without the sun all life on earth would perish. We need the sun to survive. We also need it to see where we are going. Yet we cannot look directly at the sun and sometimes we cannot even stay in the sunshine without some protection.

In the same way, we cannot behold the full glory of God but Jesus reveals God to us.

13 Walk in the Light

Aim

To rejoice in the Light of Christ.

Readings

Ephesians 5:14

Illustration

The illustration today is one of action. We will look to the candle that represents Christ in our midst and we will ask the light of Christ to shine in our lives. Then we will come forward during the singing of a hymn and receive a light.

Have a short silence, then pray:

> Blessed are you, Lord our God,
> for you have called us out of darkness
> into your bright light.
> You have called us to be children of light.
> May the brightness of your presence
> scatter all the darkness that is within us and about us.
> Grant that the lights that we receive
> may remind us of your light
> and of your love towards us,
> Jesus Christ our Lord.
> Amen.

Let everyone come the shortest way to the Christ candle and walk back by going right around the inside of the church.

Sing the hymn 'Walk in the light'.

Let the leader say, 'Receive this light and shine as lights in the world.'

14 Charging our Batteries

Aim
To show the need for prayer.

Readings
Isaiah 40:31

Illustration
It is not often you see one of these in church – a battery charger. Sometimes, even when there is fuel in the tank, the engine will not start. This is because there is no spark, no electricity to fire the engine. Then you need the battery charger. It will slowly revive the flat battery and give it new life. Then we will be able to get going again. Also a car cannot run for long without being refuelled. You need to fill it up regularly with petrol. The more miles you do, the more petrol you need.

Some of you may have battery chargers at home to charge up batteries for CD players or other things that need electricity to keep them going. Many modern torches come with a charger so that the battery can produce a bright light.

Sometimes people are a bit like a beautiful car with a full tank of petrol but a flat battery. They should be able to do all sorts but they are flat and dull or feeling run down. So many seem to lack a bright spark in their lives. When this is so, we need power from outside ourselves. Listen again to Isaiah: 'Those who wait for the Lord shall renew their strength.'

15 Natural Healing

Aim

To show that Jesus cares for the lonely, rejected and outcast.

Readings

Psalm 103:1-5

Illustration

There was a lady who lived off the west coast of Scotland on one of the islands, the island of Harris, and she had leprosy. She was forced to live alone on the seashore, where she lived off plants and shellfish. She bathed in the liquid off the shellfish and plants. All her flesh became healed and without leprosy. She praised Jesus in these words:

> There is no plant in the ground
> but is full of his virtue.
> There is no form in the strand
> but is full of his blessing.
> Jesu! Jesu! Jesu!
> Jesu! meet it were to praise him.
>
> There is no life in the sea,
> there is no creature in the river,
> there is naught in the firmament,
> but proclaims his goodness.
> Jesu! Jesu! Jesu!
> Jesu! meet it were to praise him.
>
> There is no bird on the wing,
> there is no star in the sky,
> there is nothing beneath the sun,
> but proclaims his goodness.
> Jesu! Jesu! Jesu!
> Jesu! meet it were to praise him.

16 New Every Morning

Aim

To show our God is a healing and forgiving God.

Readings

Lamentations 3:22-23

Illustration

Everybody sing 'Now, every morning is the love'; we need to take it to heart. Read verse 1. We are here awake and alive due to the love of God. During the night we have been refreshed and restored in our powers.

Read verse 2. This verse can change our lives if we take it to heart. 'New perils past': some of the things we feared yesterday did not happen or were not half as bad as we thought. 'New sins forgiven': you need to accept this. What wrongs you did before today are forgiven as long as you intend to lead a new life. You need not carry a great load of guilt around with you; guilt does not change the past but forgiveness changes the future. In the grace and goodness of God you are given a new day – learn to live it. Do not drag old sins and guilt around with you, for they will hamper your life. Start the day anew. Give thanks for the love and the healing power of God in your life. Know you are 'ransomed, healed, forgiven'. Start each day in the presence of God and with new hope in your heart: 'new thoughts of God, new hopes of heaven'.

17 God Around Us

Aim
To show that Jesus Christ was with the Father before the foundation of the world.

Readings
Acts 17:28

Illustration
There is a fountain in India with fish around it. On the fountain are words by the Indian poet Kabir: 'I laugh if I hear the fish in the sea are thirsty. I laugh if I hear man goes in search of God.'

Just think of a little fish living in a mighty ocean being told its whole life depends on water. One morning it sets out to find water. It leaves its home and travels to cold seas but it cannot find water there. It then travels south to warmer climes, still seeking, but it cannot see water there. It searches all of the seas and all this time it is restless and weary, spending much of its energy. At last it meets an old fish on the seabed and asks, 'Where is the water for I would like some?' 'Do you not know you live in the water, you move in the water, you only exist because of the water? There is no need to look for it, you are in it. If you did not have it you would die. Enjoy being in it; know that it is all around you.' This was wonderful news; there was no need to seek but there was a chance to enjoy the element in which it lived.

St Paul, when he was speaking about God to the Greeks on the Areopagus, says, 'In him we live and move and have our being' (Acts 17:28). This is a wonderful reality to discover: we need not seek God for we are in God, in his presence and in his love. Let us enjoy this reality.

18 The Promised Land

Aim

To show that Jesus is the Son of God and fulfils the longings of the law and the prophets.

Readings

Deuteronomy 8:7-10; 34:1-8

Illustration

The day before the civil rights campaigner Martin Luther King was killed by a sniper's bullet he said words of encouragement to a large crowd:

> We've got difficult days ahead. But it does not matter to me now. Because I have been to the mountain top, I won't mind. Like anyone else I would like to live a long life . . . but I am not concerned about that now. I just want to do God's will. And he's allowed me to go up the mountain. And I have looked over and seen the Promised Land. So I am happy tonight, I am not fearing any man. Mine eyes have seen the glory of the coming of the Lord.

Like Martin Luther King, if we are to survive dark days, we need to have a vision of the glory of our God.

19 Weeding and Pruning

Aim

To encourage a positive approach to Lent.

Readings

John 15:1-2
1 Corinthians 3:6-9

Illustration

Some people say they like doing what comes naturally. A man let his garden grow naturally and when asked why it was a mess he said, 'I was leaving it to God.' God will not do for us what he has given us the ability to do. If you want a good garden or a good life, you have to work at it. With the garden, if you want flowers it is no use filling the beds with vegetables. You will get out what you put in. You will get more, for you will also get weeds. If you leave your life to run itself, it will also produce weeds. Gardens and life need regular tender loving care.

Lent is a time for looking at what you have and making improvements.

In the garden some plants need splitting to give them more room to grow. You can often give away the extra to someone else. If you do not divide some plants, they will choke themselves. If we do not learn to give, we will do the same. Make room for the new in your life.

There is a constant need to weed and also to prune. Get rid of what hampers growth. Cut back on what has become rank and is taking over.

Learn to work in relationship with the soil and the climate. Learn to work in relationship with God.

Nothing is achieved without effort, without practice, without learning. If you want a good garden you have to give it priority over other things and the same is true of life.

20 Obeying God's Call

Aim
To encourage people to be faithful to their Lord.

Readings
Luke 14:26-27

Illustration
When Columbanus wanted to go and serve God as a monk his mother was not pleased. She loved him dearly and was afraid that he was wasting his life. He had lots of talent and ability. He could be someone very important in Ireland. She talked to him and tried to dissuade him, but he knew God was calling him to leave home and serve him in a monastery. His mother tried all sorts of ways to stop him. Though she loved him dearly, she was acting for Satan. Columbanus got ready to go. His mother went to the door of the house and lay down in the doorway to stop him. Columbanus was very sorry to see his mother do this, but he carefully stepped over her and went to serve God wherever God called him. In time, Columbanus did wonderful work for God in France and Italy. For a moment it would have been easy to give in and stay at home.

21 Good Rules

Aim
To show we are accountable for our actions.

Readings
Matthew 5:17-19
John 2:13-22

Illustration
There was a farmer who planned to go to France for his holidays. As he would be driving on the Continent he decided to get some practice in. He started to drive on the right-hand side of the road and to go around roundabouts anticlockwise. To say the least, he caused all sorts of trouble and had one or two close accidents. He was finally stopped by the police and charged with dangerous driving. He had broken dozens of rules in the Highway Code, and that mattered because it is written for the well-being and safety of us all. We need rules to protect us and to help us to get the best out of life. Rules are not to restrict us as much as to give us the greatest freedom within certain parameters.

What if there were no rules in a game of football? You could have as many people as you like on your team. You could pick up the ball and run or even take it home! You could make the goal-posts narrower than the football so that no one could score. But you would not have a game; you would have chaos. We need rules and standards to enjoy living together in community.

Jesus was angry with the moneychangers because they were being unjust. They were using their privileged position to make unfair demands. They were robbing people in the name of God. Jesus could not turn a blind eye. He had to act. He had to show that what was being done was not right and needed to be changed. Perhaps on a larger scene Jesus was already hinting that the time for animal sacrifices had come to an end and that a great sacrifice was about to be made in his own crucifixion.

22 Thanks, Mum

Aim

To help us to appreciate the love that is given to us through our mother.

Readings

Exodus 20:12

Illustration

By tradition this middle Sunday in Lent was a time when young children who had left home to work in a big house or on a farm were allowed home for the first time in the year. Lots of children had to work for very low wages, sometimes only their keep, and it was very hard. They missed their homes and the care of their mother. At home much had been done for them. Now they had to look after themselves. It was lovely to come home and be looked after and loved. Usually the children had little they could bring as they had little. They may have been allowed to make a cake. More often they would bring a posy of flowers they picked on the way. Perhaps the first time they had thought of giving their mother flowers and saying 'Thank you' for all that their mother had done for them. It is very easy to take our mother for granted and not notice all the work she does for us. She does this work freely, gratis, out of her own grace and goodness. What most of us learn about love, grace and goodness has its foundation in our own homes.

Do you know how much a cup of tea or coffee costs in a café? How much is a meal? What would it cost you to hire a servant to clean for you? Our mother does all this out of love. We should show we appreciate all she does and that we are truly grateful. We should never take our mother for granted or make her work more difficult. As we grow we should know we have a share in that work, because as she loves us, we love her.

23 Lazy Jack

Aim

To look at the Passion of Christ and beyond to the resurrection.

Readings

John 12:24

Illustration

Lazy Jack was given a sack of grain. His task was to sow the seed for the village so that they would have a harvest in the autumn. Jack looked at the seed. It was golden and beautiful. He thought it would be a shame to bury it in the ground. So he took it home and put it in a cupboard. No one knew that he had not sown the seed. Jack took it easy. It was only later in the year when there were no shoots, no signs of new wheat growing, that the village realised there was something wrong. Obviously the seed was not in the ground. After a search they found it in Lazy Jack's cupboard. The mice had eaten some, but most of it was still intact. Jack had almost allowed a community to starve by not sowing the seed. Like much in our lives, it was a case of use it or lose it. The villagers put the seed in the ground – it was late for sowing but they trusted in the power within the seed to grow and it did. In the end nothing was lost and the harvest was good.

24 Victory

Aim
To rejoice in the resurrection and in the presence of the risen Lord.

Readings
1 Corinthians 15:57

Illustration
Napoleon escaped from his island prison. His armies regathered under the French flag and Europe was plunged into war. The British army under Wellington landed in Belgium and prepared to fight near a small village called Waterloo. There was no way of communicating to England the news except by semaphore. Day after day a man watched from the tower of Winchester Cathedral, peering towards the south coast. On a misty day the watcher received a message: 'Wellington defeated.' The mist came down and a sadness filled Winchester and spread over England. The watcher stayed at his post. After a long while the mist lifted and the message was repeated: 'Wellington defeated.' But now two more words were added and they made a great difference: 'Wellington defeated the French.' The assumed defeat was a victory. A new message sped to London. Bells rang out and flags flew. The message, which seemed one of defeat, was in fact the start of the news of victory. Likewise we must move from the crucifixion to the joy of the resurrection. We are able to proclaim, 'Death is conquered. We are free. Christ has won the victory.'

Jesus defeated/death

We are free

Christ has won the victory.

25 The Breath of Life

Aim
To share in the wonder of the resurrection.

Readings
1 Corinthians 15:45
John 20:22

Illustration
Suddenly a man fell to the ground. He had stopped breathing and it would not be long before he was totally dead. But help was at hand. Someone was willing to give him mouth-to-mouth resuscitation. They breathed their breath into him, filling his lungs, and then helped his lungs to expel the air and then receive some more breath. This process went on for a while at ten breaths a minute; without it the man would have died. By the time the ambulance came the man was breathing freely on his own. The person had saved his life. Jesus breathes new life into us and gives us eternal life. Jesus defeats death and brings us to eternal life.

(You may be able to get a St John's Ambulance person or a paramedic to offer to demonstrate 'Breath of Life' – they also provide a useful card with this title.)

26 The Light of Life

Aim
To rejoice in the presence of the risen Lord.

Readings
John 8:12

Illustration
Have you ever been caught in the fog? The whole world becomes cold and grey. Vision is greatly restricted. Everything around appears to be dull and damp. Then suddenly there is a shining, an extra amount of light; there is a radiance that begins to appear all around. The sun breaks through and the fog lifts and disappears. The day seems so glorious and bright. This was the experience of the disciples with the resurrection. They shut themselves in and shut the fullness of life out. They were locked in by sorrow and fear. They just wanted to hide. It was then he came. He came because he was needed. He came back from the dead. He came to be with them. He came to guide them. He came to help them. He came to be friends. He came to transform their world. He comes now and he comes to us. He comes to chase away our darkness and fear and to make our world bright.

27 The Good Shepherd

Aim

To show how much the Good Shepherd cares for us and will do for us.

Readings

John 10:1-18

Illustration

There was a group of shepherds who often talked about caring for their sheep. Yet, when trouble came, some did not want to bother; others said the sheep were not worth the risk; one or two took the money and left. One could be heard saying, 'You cannot believe a lamb is worth the life of a shepherd.' The reply from a hired man was, 'Of course it is not.'

Listening to all this was the good shepherd. It made him sad to think that the sheep were not truly loved. He loved his sheep dearly and would do anything to save them. Suddenly an old man came to him and said, 'I have been looking at your flock and you have a ewe lamb missing. She has wandered off and is in danger of death.' The shepherd left the comfort of home and the safety of his surroundings and began the search. Some were sure he should not have bothered. There were plenty of other sheep; why bother with a wayward one? The shepherd's life was more precious than the lamb's. The shepherd was soon travelling dark valleys. More than once he was at risk himself. Briars tore at his hands and his feet. There was a gaping hole in his side. Thorns had pierced his head. He was calling the lamb by name. At last there was a weak response. It was down a steep slope and in danger of falling further. The shepherd did not fear but descended into the depths. The darkness was trying to hold on to the lamb. The shepherd reached into the thorn bushes and became entangled; he was caught alongside the lamb. Even now he reached out to comfort it. There he lay, life ebbing out of him. He was trapped for more than 48 hours. But on the third day he broke free and rising up brought the lamb with him. He carried it all the way home. When they saw him they rejoiced. 'Just see how much he loves his flock and what he was willing to suffer for one little ewe lamb.'

28 Evangelism

Aim

To show we are one with Christ and that we are called to bear fruit.

Readings

Acts 8:4+, 26-40
Isaiah 53

Illustration

We hear little of the disciples after the resurrection but we know they all bore the fruit of being with Jesus. After the death of Stephen, the disciples scattered because of persecution. We know Philip went to Samaria and told the story of Jesus. He preached of the love of God. Through the disciples the Church was growing rapidly and beyond the boundaries of Jerusalem (see Acts 8:4+). Peter and John also went to the Samaritans.

A road from Jerusalem went by Bethlehem and, just south of Gaza, joined the main road to Egypt and beyond. St Luke points out that this is the Old or Desert Gaza, not the more modern one. Along this road travelled the Chancellor of the Exchequer of the queen of Ethiopia. He had been to Jerusalem to worship. He is at least a seeker of God. He was in his chariot reading Isaiah 53. Philip simply asked if he understood what he was reading. The Ethiopian said how could he without a guide? Philip was invited into the chariot and they looked at the words: 'He was led like a lamb to the slaughter.' Philip talked of Jesus of the crucifixion and resurrection. The Ethiopian was moved and wanted to be baptised in the nearby water. After being baptised the Ethiopian went on his way rejoicing. Again we see Philip bearing fruit as he does the work of Jesus. Tradition has it that the Ethiopian went home and started to evangelise Ethiopia. And through the witness of many the Church grew in the faith and in number.

29 Love's Explosion

Aim

To know that we are chosen by God.

Readings

John 1:4-5
1 Thessalonians 4:16-17

Illustration

Once upon a time there was an explosion that radiated out through the world. Countless people were touched, infected: many found it contagious as someone who was already touched passed it on to them. The explosion happened on a hill called Calvary just outside Jerusalem. Here love broke out in great power, defeating darkness. In a flash of blinding love, the Christ released a new way of life for the world. The love of God radiated through the whole earth and all times. The results of that explosion are still being felt today because he who died rose again. He lives and seeks to share his love with us. He comes to us and wants to be our friend. There are always those who will protect themselves against such an event; who will ignore his presence and avoid his radiant love. But he will transform all who come to be touched and give them the power to become the true children of God. They will shine with his presence and his love.

30 Rescued from Above

Aim

To rejoice in the presence of the ascended Lord.

Readings

Psalm 18:16-19

Illustration

At first there was a silence, as if we had been left to our own devices. Through our foolishness we had been caught by a rising tide. We had sent up a plea, by means of a telephone in the refuge box that was placed on stilts above the waves. Some caring people had built this place of comparative safety on the sands to accommodate fools who disobeyed the guidelines of safe crossings.

Suddenly there was a whirring sound from on high. It was no vision. It was a Sea King helicopter. A man was coming down from the safety of the helicopter and being lowered to where we were. He was very friendly. He did not tell us off. He did not say he came to admire the scenery! He said to each of us in turn, 'Do not worry. You will be all right. Fasten yourself to me.' Once one of us was fastened to him he signalled to the helicopter above and we were raised to safety. He came down four times altogether. He told us sometimes he was actually dropped into a raging sea to pick someone up. His purpose was always the same: he came down that we might be lifted up; he descended that we might ascend with him. Then we were taken to dry land. I looked back on my poor old car with water flowing almost over its roof. It would be a write-off. But we were safe. A little like the resurrection of the body and our being lifted to heaven. Words of Psalm 18:16-19 came to mind: 'He reached down from on high, he took me; he drew me out of mighty waters . . . He brought me out into a broad place: he delivered me because he delighted in me.'

Jesus came down that we might be raised up on high.

31 Oliver's Request

Aim

To show the importance of knowing Jesus personally.

Readings

Hebrews 7:19b, 25

Illustration

In the film *Oliver!*, Oliver Twist is in the poorhouse with many other young people. They want someone to complain that they are hungry and want more food. In this case no one wants to do it for they know they are likely to be punished. They decided to pick straws and whoever draws the shortest straw has to do it. If you draw the shortest straw, it means you are chosen. Oliver draws the shortest straw. The others have elected him. So though he is frightened, he goes to the front and asks for more. 'Please Sir, I would like some more.' In the poorhouse this is unthinkable and, as the young people expected, Oliver is punished for asking.

32 Sufficient Energy

Aim

To rejoice in the presence and power of the Spirit.

Readings

Acts 1:8
Isaiah 40:31

Illustration

One of Europe's leading ecologists has said the energy crisis we face is not so much in energy supplies but in our own thinking. There is enough energy in the ebb and flow of the tides, in the running of rivers, in the winds and in the rays of the sun to supply our needs if we would give time and attention to these. Three things are obvious:

(1) Many energy supplies are limited and will run out.

(2) Wrong thinking or lack of proper attention makes us do nothing.

(3) All around there is power that we do not realise.

Too often the Church tries to go along in its own resources and strength, and it can be seen to be running out of supplies. We spend too much of our attention looking in the wrong direction.

The power of God is here, for the Lord is here: His Spirit is with us.

We need to learn to wait upon the Lord and the power of his might.

33 The Greatness of God

Aim
To encourage a greater awareness of the Trinity.

Readings
Psalm 145:3
Romans 11:33-36

Illustration
A child went down to the beach and dug a hole in the sand. She then went down to the sea and brought some water to fill the hole. In a moment the water disappeared. She went back for more water, and then more. But the same thing happened each time. The little girl became exhausted and began to cry. Meanwhile the tide had been coming in. Her father showed her how to make a channel for the sea, so that it would flow naturally into the hole and fill it. We are like the little girl: we try to fill our minds with ideas about God and often exhaust ourselves. We talk too much. We need learn to wait upon God, knowing he will come to us. Trying to understand the Trinity is like trying to pour the whole sea into a small hole. Yet we can rest in the Trinity and enjoy the love of Father, Son and Holy Spirit.

34 Abusing the Rules

Aim

To show that lives are richer than the keeping of rules – but that rules are necessary.

Readings

Matthew 5:19; 23:23-24

Illustration

Rules and regulations are there to help us and the society we live in. Occasionally you hear of some absurd application of the law, usually by someone who says something like, 'It's more than my job's worth.' A young motorcyclist was knocked off his bike in an area of parking meters. His bike was put carefully at the side of the road. Even though the traffic warden knew of the event, he placed a parking ticket on the bike. Fortunately, the city council was more understanding when a plea was made. Some people find it very hard to understand that rules are there to help us rather than hinder us.

35 Risk

Aim

To show how Jesus risked safety and security for us.

Readings

Mark 3:1-6

Illustration

Jesus risked his own safety and security for us. As Christians, we are often called to share in this risky adventure. The call is often like the call to the man with the withered hand: 'Come forward . . . stretch out' (Mark 3:3, 5).

Very often the Church hides behind set services and conventions. The words and the patterns are fixed so that no one is disturbed. Jesus calls, 'Come forward.' Stand where everyone can see you. Where every fault-finding eye can fall upon you. Where those who reject Jesus can vent themselves upon you. 'Safety first' is not our policy: the Church is not meant to be hidden – 'Come forward' for Jesus. Then 'stretch out', even if you feel your talent has withered. Attempt the impossible for God, trusting in his power. Take risks for God and let him work through you. The call of Jesus to the man with the withered hand is a call to the Church to let him work through us. Come forward . . . stretch out.

36 Sowing Seed

Aim

To show that the kingdom of God is waiting to grow in us.

Readings

Matthew 13:3

Illustration

Jonathan Chapman used to travel around farms in America with his Bible. In the evenings he would read to the family; not many of them could read themselves. They looked forward to his visits and they called him 'Johnny Appleseed'.

This is how he got his nickname. On some farms he noticed the men busy making cider. The apples were pressed and when the juice was extracted the pips were thrown away. 'What a waste,' thought Johnny: those little pips could grow into fine trees. So Johnny asked if he could have some seed. The man replied he could have as much seed as he wanted. Johnny filled his saddlebag with seeds. When he visited a farm, in the evening he read from the Bible, then before he left he would make some holes in the soil and plant some apple seeds. He then made a little fence around them to protect them and to give them the chance to grow. For over 40 years Johnny did this work, sowing the word of God in the hearts of people and sowing apple seeds in the ground. Everywhere he went he left something behind to give pleasure and nourishment to the farming people. He understood well that seeds could not grow unless they were planted.

37 The Power of the Lord

Aim
To learn to turn to Jesus in the storms of life.

Readings
Mark 4:35-41

Illustration
Do you know the story of Aladdin and his lamp? The lamp had wonderful powers but most people did not recognise it. The lamp standing unused was no better than any other. It could give out a little light but its great power remained untapped. It is no use having a wonderful power if you do not use it. In the same way, it is no use saying you believe in a Saviour if you do not call upon him.

Too often we allow Jesus to sleep in our lives. We struggle on alone and are often overwhelmed because we do not call upon him in the storm. While we allow fear to mount and energies to be overpowered, we fail to call upon the greatest power, which is our Lord.

In the storms of fear and sorrow, when we are feeling overwhelmed, we need to know the presence and the power of our God. We need to know again that God can bring order out of chaos and that Christ can give us his peace. Do not let Jesus sleep in your life; call upon him each day. Take heed these words from Julian of Norwich:

He said not: 'Thou shalt not be tempest-tossed; thou shalt not be work-weary; thou shalt not be distressed.' But he did say: 'Thou shalt not be overcome.'

38 Contact

Aim
To show Jesus is the giver of hope and life.

Readings
Mark 5:30

Illustration
How often do we lose contact with friends because we do not make the effort? To maintain a relationship with anyone we need to meet them and talk to them. If they are far away we can at least write, telephone or send an e-mail. A once-a-year Christmas card could hardly be called contact.

In a car the contacts give a vital spark that fires the engine. If the contacts are broken, the engine will not fire properly. Even if we have plenty of fuel and the battery is charged, the car will not go if there are no contacts at work.

When Jesus asks, 'Who touched me?' could you say, 'It was I, Lord'? Do you keep in proper contact with Jesus? When the woman touched him, power travelled from Jesus to her. We so often fail to achieve because we go it alone and do not touch base with Jesus.

(You might like to use the hymn 'What a friend we have in Jesus'; let the people read it during a silence.)

39 Freedom

Aim

To show Jesus has work for us but will not force himself or his work upon us.

Readings

Revelation 3:20

Illustration

In the totalitarian state you are not allowed free choice. You must do as you are told. If you do not open your door to the officials, it will be broken down. You cannot hide because they will seek you out and make you do what they want.

Jesus is different. He has the power but he will not force himself upon you. The choice is yours: he respects your free will. You can edge him out of your life and home if you so choose. You can be too busy to bother to keep in contact with him if you so desire. He will not force you.

Have a large print of Holman Hunt's picture 'The Light of the World'. If you look at it you will see the door has not been opened for a long time. Jesus stands there knocking and waiting to bring his light upon those who live within. There is no means of opening the door from the outside. If he is to enter, you have to let him in. It is good to think of these words of Jesus every day: 'Behold, I stand at the door and knock' (Revelation 3:20).

40 The Gift of the Kingdom

Aim

To compare the rule of Herod with the rule of Jesus.

Readings

Luke 12:32

Illustration

So many rulers rule by force. They often think of their subjects as objects for their own selfish ends. If people do not obey, there are ways of dealing with them, which include torture, imprisonment and even death. Dictators throughout history have got rid of those who opposed them by exterminating them; there are many tyrannical governments in our world that still operate like this.

The kingdom of heaven is the free gift of God's presence and love to us. It is not forced upon us but is offered freely. God loves us before we even turn to him. We are not rejected from his kingdom. We leave it of our own free will when we do not obey the King in love.

41 Seeking the Lost

Aim

To show that we need times of quietness and rest.

Readings

Luke 15:4-7

Illustration

There was a famous General who met a poor shepherd. The shepherd was distressed because he had lost a lamb and could not find it. The General offered to help and sent his soldiers in search of the lamb. One by one the soldiers returned to camp hungry, muddied and feeling too tired to carry on. It was dark by then and they felt they could do nothing more. The next morning, just as it was getting light, the General was seen coming into the camp carrying the lamb under his greatcoat to keep it warm. This is what made him such a great leader: he was not put off and he did not think of himself too much. He only stopped looking for the lamb when he found it. (You can compare this to the Good Shepherd.)

42 Is It Worth the Effort?

Aim
To show the care and concern of Jesus.

Readings
Matthew 10:42

Illustration
There is a story about a boy walking along a beach. All along the shore there were thousands of starfish washed up. You could hardly walk on the sand for them. The boy was putting a few in his bucket and taking them back to the sea. A man came along and said, 'There are thousands of starfish stranded. Why do you bother? You will hardly make an impression. You will only be able to put a few back into the sea.' The boy replied. 'It will matter for these few and it will matter to me.'

Though our effort may be small, it is counted as worthwhile, and who knows what God will do with it?

43 Full or Empty?

Aim
To see Jesus as the Bread of Life.

Readings
John 6:27
Luke 12:15
Matthew 4:4

Illustration
Throughout our world there are people who seem to have to fill their lives with food, with things or with activity. No matter how much they get, they are still not satisfied. When young people say they are bored, it is usually when they have plenty happening around them but they recognise emptiness within. Bored means having a hole drilled in you. There is something in you that things cannot fill, no matter how you stuff yourself or your days. God made us for himself and nothing else will really fill the space he created within us for himself. In each of us there is a space for the eternal and nothing less than the eternal God can fill it.

44 Dying of Analysis

Aim
To show the calling of God and the stalling of our hearts.

Readings
Psalm 63:1
Acts 17:28
John 6:35, 41-51

Illustration
There was a brilliant scientist who was keen on analysis. He wanted to get to the basic elements of everything. A meal was set before him and he was hungry. But he wanted to check where this food came from and what was in it. He went into his laboratory and started on a loaf of bread. He did not eat any. He checked what its constituents were. He discovered wholemeal flour, water, yeast, vegetable fat, preservatives, emulsifiers and vinegar. He checked out the preservatives and found calcium propionate and potassium sorbate. By now he was starving but research must go on. The emulsifiers kept him busy for ages. He found mono- and diacetyl tartaric acid, esters of mono- and diglycerides, fatty acids. He was kept very busy but he grew weaker and weaker. He still had to analyse the wholemeal and check out the grains. Sadly he died of starvation whilst looking at the loaf. There was food all around him but he died of analysis.

45 Shining in the Dark

Aim
To seek to abide in Jesus and let him abide in us.

Readings
2 Corinthians 4:6
Ephesians 5:8

Illustration
There was once a man who bought a beautiful box for his wife. The box had flowers on the top and they would glow in the dark. As it was for her birthday he hid it away in a drawer and left it there for a few weeks. On her birthday it was given to her all wrapped in a lovely parcel. She was delighted and could hardly wait until the evening. When it got dark she looked at the box but it did not shine; it had not changed at all. They both waited until it got really dark but the box never did shine. They felt a little cheated because the box was bought to shine. Then a little note fell from the packaging. It said, 'If you want me to shine all night, you need put me in the sun all day.' The box would only glow if it was left out in the daylight. They left it out all the next day and, true to the words, all night it glowed with a splendid light.

If we are to glow with eternal life, we need to be placed in the presence of the Son of God to let him abide in us and for us to know we abide in him.

46 A Faithful Helper

Aim

To affirm our commitment to Christ.

Readings

Deuteronomy 31:6
John 14:18

Illustration

Here is a story of loyalty. A man and his dog walked in the hill country. The man saw an old mine in a hillside and went in. Whilst inside, the roof collapsed and trapped the man by his leg. For a while the dog stayed with him but it then went outside the mine and stood at the entrance. There it began to howl to attract attention. No one took any notice at first. The dog became hungry and thirsty but it did not leave its post. The weather became bad; the dog got wet and cold but it stayed put and continued to howl. Finally a nearby farmer decided there was something wrong with the dog and he climbed the hillside to find it. When he arrived, the dog stopped howling but would not let him touch it or even feed it. It tried to lead him into the mine. The farmer made to go away but as soon as he did this the dog started to howl and to walk towards the mine again. At last he decided to go to the entrance and call to see if there was anyone there. He heard a voice and so went cautiously inside. He saw the man was trapped and went for help. The dog seemed to understand because it now stayed with its master and remained with him until help came and he was rescued.

47 Prayer and Hypocrisy

Aim

To make sure our traditions do not hinder our relationship with God.

Readings

Matthew 6:5-6

Illustration

A devout Muslim carries his prayer mat around with him and prays a fixed number of times each day. At the fixed times he will unroll his mat and turn to God. This is a wonderful way of keeping in contact with his creator.

There was a certain Muslim who had great anger in his heart. He was in hot pursuit of a man whom he wanted to kill. He had a dagger and was intent on murder. Suddenly the call to prayer rang out from the mosque. The man stopped for a moment, rushed his prayers, then continued on his murderous chase. The prayer was part of his daily ritual but he did not let it touch his heart. This man could be seen to be a hypocrite.

48 A Godless Church

Aim

To encourage our church to be open and welcoming.

Readings

James 2:1-5

Illustration

There was once a very famous church. Every Sunday it was fashionable to go there and be seen. People came in their finery. Some of the most important people of the land attended it. The music and the choir were superb, the ordering of the service was of a very high standard; everything done was to the highest degree of excellence and in the best possible taste. For a good few Sundays a poorly dressed and shabby-looking person turned up at the door but was turned away for one reason or another. After a few weeks of trying to get in, the woman sat on the lowest step and prayed to God, 'Lord, why can I not get entrance into this church?' The Lord replied, 'My daughter, how do I know? I have been trying to get into this church for years.'

49 Obeying the Vision

Aim
To encourage a personal relationship with Christ the living Lord.

Readings
Acts 26:19
Mark 3:31-35
Luke 2:48-50

Illustration
In his poem 'Gareth and Lynette', Tennyson tells of the struggle Gareth has to leave home. He wants to become one of the knights of Arthur but his mother does not want him to leave home. She has already lost two of her sons to Arthur's court. 'Hast thou no pity on my loneliness?' she asks. 'Stay, my best son, ye are yet more a boy than a man,' she pleads. The mother produces excellent reasons for Gareth to stay at home and ignore his vision. Here, the tempter is using someone who loves him dearly to stop Gareth serving his vision. Gareth replies:

O Mother,
How can you keep me tethered to you – Shame.
A grown man I am, a man's work I must do.
Follow the deer? Follow Christ the King,
Live pure, speak true, right wrong, follow the King –
Else, wherefore born.

Gareth was not tempted through his mother but followed the vision as he saw it.

50 The Fourth Wise Man

Aim
To show that Jesus calls us to serve each other rather than to lord it over people.

Readings
Matthew 25:34-40

Illustration
There is a story about a fourth wise man who wanted to come and see the Christ. He started off well. He dressed in his best clothes, rode a fine horse and brought a present of precious stones. On his journey he met a group of poor people who were hungry, so he gave away half of his jewels for them to trade for food. Then he met a family who were taken into slavery because of a debt. He used the rest of his precious jewels to buy their freedom. Further on he found a merchant in deep distress. His horse had died on him and he would not get his goods to be sold on time. The generous wise man gave him his horse and all its trappings. Now he had to walk on foot and the going was slow.

He was old and very weary. He wondered if he would ever see the Christ. The way was very muddy and he met a young family trying to get their cart out of the mud. The wise man helped them but ended up very dirty. He now wondered if he should give up and go home. In a dream he was told, 'The Christ you seek is now only a little distance away. He will welcome you because he knows you. You have met him many times on your journey in the poor and the needy. You soiled your clothes in caring for him. Tomorrow you will meet him and he will welcome you.' And so it was.

51 Hospitality

Aim
To express the unity of all believers, as there is only 'One Church, one faith, one Lord'.

Readings
Genesis 18:1-15
Hebrews 13:2

Illustration
Hospitality was of great importance in the ancient world. By being open to others, the great Other, who is God, was given the opportunity to enter into your life. See the example of Abraham and Sarah when visited by the Lord (Genesis 18:1-15). In the story it is hard to decide whether we are dealing with three men, three angels or the three-person God. Ask the congregation who visited Abraham: was it men, angels, God? (Be careful how you phrase the question for it is not an 'either/or'. All visited Abraham at Mamre. The person that replies 'Yes' to the question or says, 'All three' would get top marks!)

There is a Celtic poem which expresses the Other approaching us through others.

> I saw a stranger yestere'en
> I put food in the eating place,
> drink in the drinking place,
> music in the listening place
> and in the sacred name of the Triune
> he blessed myself and my house,
> my cattle and my dear ones,
> and the lark said in her song
> often, often, often,
> goes the Christ in a stranger's guise.

52 Unheeded Warning

Aim
To show that our relationships are important.

Readings
Psalm 8

Illustration
Once a bird flying high overhead saw how our world was becoming polluted. The bird saw the rubbish dumped into the sea and fish struggling to survive, great tracts of land being robbed of trees, the ice-caps slowly melting. So it decided that it must tell the humans about what was happening. The first group would not listen – well, who would believe a bird! The next group were making good profits and did not want anything to be disturbed. A third group said they would happily talk about it for years. No one wanted to do anything. Yet the bird knew that all things were linked together. If the humans destroyed the environment, all the birds and all the animals would also suffer. Why were the humans so insensitive to their surroundings and to each other? The bird learnt that the humans had lost a sense of awe and wonder because they had broken their relationship with the Creator God. If they would not listen to the cries of creation, if they would not listen to the voice of God, they were not likely to hear a bird.

53 Self-giving

Aim

To show that God wants all of us and not just gifts and prayers.

Readings

1 Corinthians 13:3

Illustration

Imagine a table. I want you to put on it all the things you want to give to God: your time, talents, money; your home, your friends, your loved ones; your job, your plans, your future.

You are going to need a great big table. We raise up the things we want to give to God and say, 'All things come from you, O God, and of your own do we give you.'

But wait, one thing that God wants is still missing. Who knows what it is?

GOD WANTS YOU.

More than any gift, more than gold or silver, God wants you.

God wants you to give yourself to him.

God wants you to give your love.

God wants you more than anything.

St Paul said, 'If I give away all my possessions . . . but do not have love, I gain nothing' (1 Corinthians 13:3).

54 Serving the Poor

Aim

To compare the ambition of James and John and the servant role of Jesus.

Readings

Proverbs 14:31; 19:17

Illustration

When Toyohiko Kagawa, who lived in Japan, met Christianity he was captured by its call to serve. He prayed, 'O God, make me like Christ.' To become like Christ he went to live in the slums of Kobe to care for others. He chose to live in a shed that was about two metres square. On the very first night he was asked to share his room and bed with a man with a contagious itch, the first test of his aim to serve. He welcomed the poor man. Then a beggar asked for his shirt and he gave it. The next day the beggar came back for Kagawa's coat and trousers. Kagawa gave them and was left wearing a ragged kimono. At first the slum dwellers laughed at him but they soon came to admire him. Kagawa wrote:

> God dwells in the lowliest of men. He sits on the dust heap among the prison convicts. He stands with the juvenile delinquents. He is there with the beggars. He is among the sick; he stands with the unemployed. Therefore let him who would meet God visit the prison cell before going to the temple. Before he goes to church let him visit the hospital. Before he reads the Bible let him visit the beggar.

55 The Blind Leading the Blind

Aim
To show that Jesus opens our eyes to the reality of the world.

Readings
Luke 6:39

Illustration
The comic character Mr Magoo is funny because he is short-sighted, though in real life he would be a tragic person. He walks across crocodiles thinking they are logs. He steps out of a window in high-rise flats just as a window cleaner's hoist reaches the window. He steps off the side of a pier as a boat pulls level alongside. He does not come to harm but he often leaves a trail of chaos and disaster behind him.

Can we see what is happening around us, to our communities and the way we are shaping the future? Or are we content to leave it in the hands of those who are blind to many of the finer things of life? If we allow the blind to lead us, will we not both fall into the ditch?

It is of extreme importance that we make sure we are led by men and women of vision. It is no use having a quick fix or a laugh now if we are destroying our future. Pray for vision for yourself and your leaders.

56 Lantern Saints

Aim

To rejoice in God's saints.

Readings

Matthew 5:16

Illustration

The Lantern Saints were a group of early Methodists who lived on the North Yorkshire Moors. They had a meeting place on one of the highest points of the moor at Trough House at the head of Fryup Dale. And people came from outlying farms and hamlets, from the dales of Westerdale, Danby Dale, Farndale, Glaisdale, Rosedale and Great and Little Fryup. It made Trough House look like the centre of a web that spread out into each moorland valley. Often in the winter they struggled up to the moorland height and met in a shuttered room. As each family entered they would light their lantern (a good symbol of receiving the light of the Gospel and the Light of Christ). Once the service was over they would set off in every direction. You could see the light they had received and carried with them travelling to each dale, to farms and homes. From that light they would see in the dark and light other lights. This light was a symbol of how they sought to live by the Light of Christ. These ordinary folk were rightly known locally as the 'Lantern Saints'.

57 True Love

Aim
To encourage love of God and of each other.

Readings
Matthew 22:36-39; 19:21-22

Illustration
My Dearest,

I love you with all my heart.

I think of you every minute of the day.

I would do anything for you. I would swim shark-infested rivers to get to you. I would climb the steepest of mountains. I would travel the whole earth to be with you. I would brave fire and frost, wind and hail to be at your side.

But I cannot see you this week. I was coming tonight but it is too cold and damp for me to bother. Tomorrow I have fitness training and I am out with the lads the day after. I have a new computer game I want to try out on Wednesday, and a match to go to on Thursday. Friday as ever is swimming, and on Saturday the finals are on the television. I would do anything for you but it is a busy week. Sorry.

Keep in touch,

Yours always.

Not what I would call a promising relationship but is this the way we often deal with God and our prayers? Do we really love the Lord with all our heart?

58 Opportunity

Aim

To show that God calls each of us and we all have an opportunity to answer that call.

Readings

Mark 1:16-20

Illustration

The need to react to God's call is caught well in Shakespeare's *Julius Caesar*, Act IV:

> There is a tide in the affairs of men,
> Which, taken at the flood leads on to fortune;
> Omitted, all the voyage of their life
> Is bound in shallows and in miseries.
> On such a full sea we are now afloat,
> And we must take the current when it serves,
> Or lose our ventures.

Fortunately, our God will call us again and again. There is a time when we have to stop talking about Christ and set out to follow him.

Jesus calls us, whoever we are.

There was once a very ordinary man (if there is such a being) called Aeshines, who came to Socrates and said, 'I am a poor man. I have nothing to give you but myself.' Socrates replied, 'Do you not see that you are giving me the most precious thing of all?'

Jesus wants the gift of ourselves far more than talk and theory. Will we truly seek to follow him?

59 Don't be Alarmed

Aim

To know that whatever happens in this world or to us, God is always with us and promises us the victory through Jesus Christ our Lord.

Readings

Matthew 24:6

Illustration

When you go to an airport there are two places with frightening names. There is the 'departure lounge' and the 'terminal'. One is for those who are departing from us and the other is where it all ends! Well, you could look at it that way. Sometimes the departure lounge is a sad place because we are seeing people off whom we might not see again for a long time. But usually it is full of excited people who are going on holiday or going somewhere special. When we come to the terminal, it is not that we are going to stop there. It can be where all traffic is halted but we are going on to a better place. We are not going to stop at the terminal.

I tell you this because Jesus was talking about the end of the world, as we know it. He was pointing out that there are certain signs that point us towards what seems to be the end. But for us it is the beginning of something new. All the troubles are but the birth pangs of the coming of the kingdom. It is easy to quake with fear when we do not know what lies ahead. But we do know who is waiting to meet us. We may fear that we are losing round after round of the battle but in Christ Jesus we are assured the victory will be ours. The terminal will be where we move on to a better kingdom.

60 Under Control

Aim
To show that Christ is King and seeks to rule in our hearts.

Readings
Matthew 24:7-14
Romans 8:18-23, 35-39

Illustration
The school bus is at the top of a steep hill when the driver slumps at the wheel. The bus starts to swerve all over the road and is picking up speed. There is general panic on the bus for it is out of control. Two lads rush forward and move the driver off the seat. A girl grabs the steering wheel and gently applies the brakes. She has never driven before but knows what to do. One minute everything was out of control and the next the busload of children was rescued by the quick thinking and acting of three young people.

The world seems to have a tendency to run out of control; wars and rumours of wars, famine and earthquakes, violence and force seem to take over. Jesus warned us that these things would happen but that we should see them as the birth pangs of the new age, the coming of God's kingdom. We should celebrate that God is in control, that Christ is our Redeemer and King.

Topical Index

Numbers refer to Illustrations and not to pagination.

Bible Reference Index

Numbers refer to Illustrations and not to pagination.